THANK YOU GOD!
Wonderful World of Animals Coloring Book

THANK YOU GOD!
My First Animal Atlas Coloring Book

© 2022 by Dr. Diana Carle
Nature's Living Classroom Publishing
For Information Contact:
Dr. Diana Carle at www.DoctorDianaCarle.com
Written and illustrated by Dr. Diana Carle
Edited by Dr. Frank Carle and Kristina Carle

I give all glory and thanks to God for the gifts of teaching, writing, and illustrating to be able to create this book because every good gift comes from Him through Christ Jesus our Lord, Amen!

A special dedication to precious little Nate.
I hope you grow up loving the wonderous animals of God's creation and knowing God's amazing love for you!

Genesis 1:20-23

20 Then God said, "Let the waters teem with swarms of living creatures, and let birds fly above the earth in the open expanse of the heavens." 21 And God created the great sea creatures and every living creature that moves, with which the waters swarmed, according to their kind, and every winged bird according to its kind; and God saw that it was good. 22 God blessed them, saying, "Be fruitful and multiply, and fill the waters in the seas, and let birds multiply on the earth." 23 And there was evening and there was morning, a fifth day.

Genesis 1:24-25

24 Then God said, "Let the earth produce living creatures according to their kind: livestock and crawling things and animals of the earth according to their kind"; and it was so. 25 God made the animals of the earth according to their kind, and the livestock according to their kind, and everything that crawls on the ground according to its kind; and God saw that it was good.

Thank You God for Creating the World!

The Bible tells us that God created the lands and waters and all the animals that live in them! We call the biggest masses of land **CONTINENTS**, where deer and other animals suited for life on land live.

We call the biggest masses of water that separate the continents, **OCEANS**, where fish and other creatures suited for life in water live.

We can count 1, 2, 3, 4, 5, 6, 7... That makes **SEVEN** biggest masses of land that we call **CONTINENTS**. The **CONTINENTS** are named: North America, South America, Europe, Asia, Africa, Australia, and Antarctica.

We can count 1, 2, 3, 4, 5...

That makes **FIVE** biggest bodies of water that we call **OCEANS**. The **OCEANS** are named: Atlantic Ocean, Pacific Ocean, Southern Ocean, Arctic Ocean, and Indian Ocean.

Thank You God for Making a Special Home for Each and Every Animal!

Each continent is *so* special with its own unique characteristics that make it just the right place for certain animals to live.

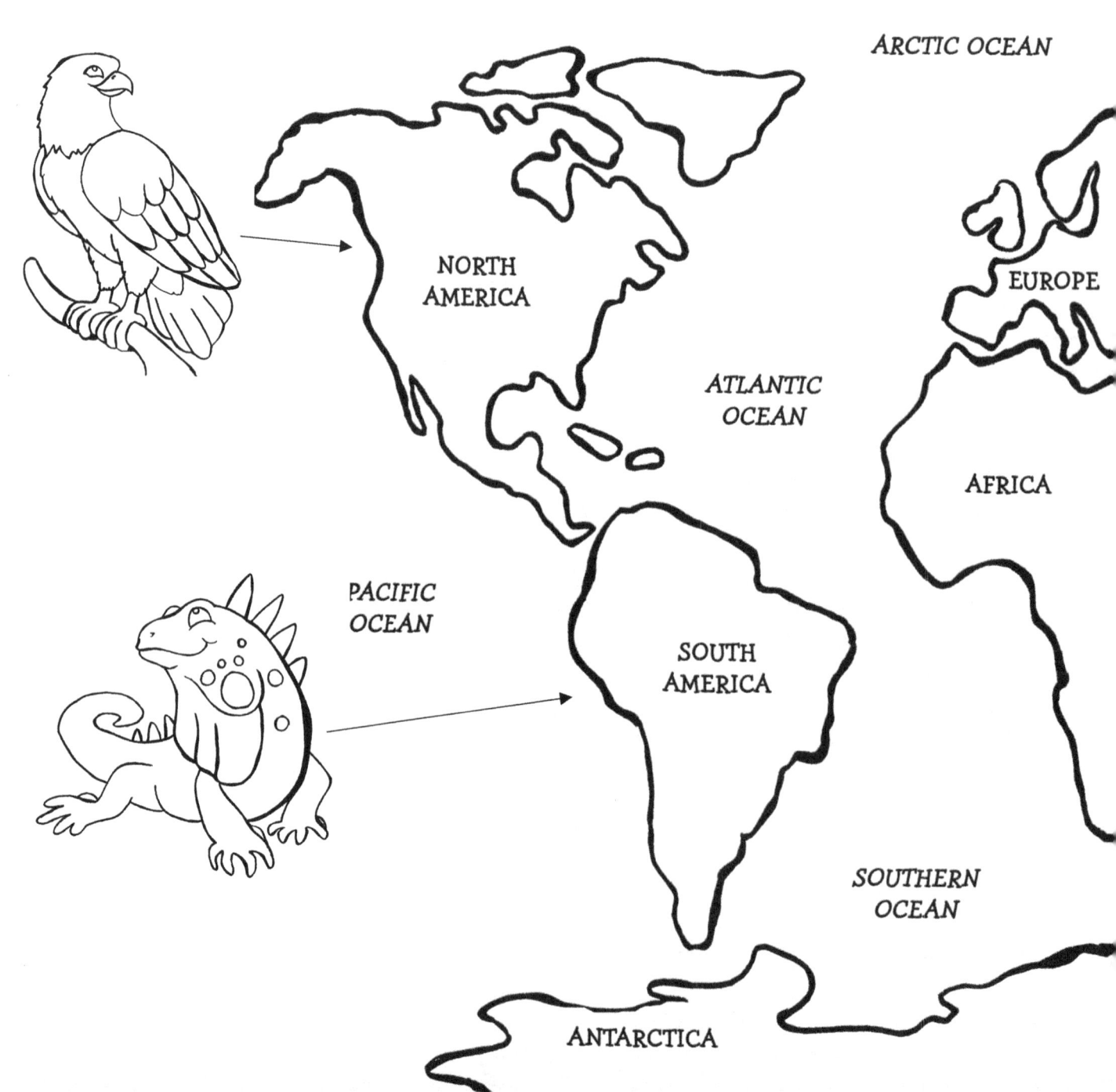

We are going to explore just some of these unique animals and the continents where they live, as well as the animals that live in the oceans.

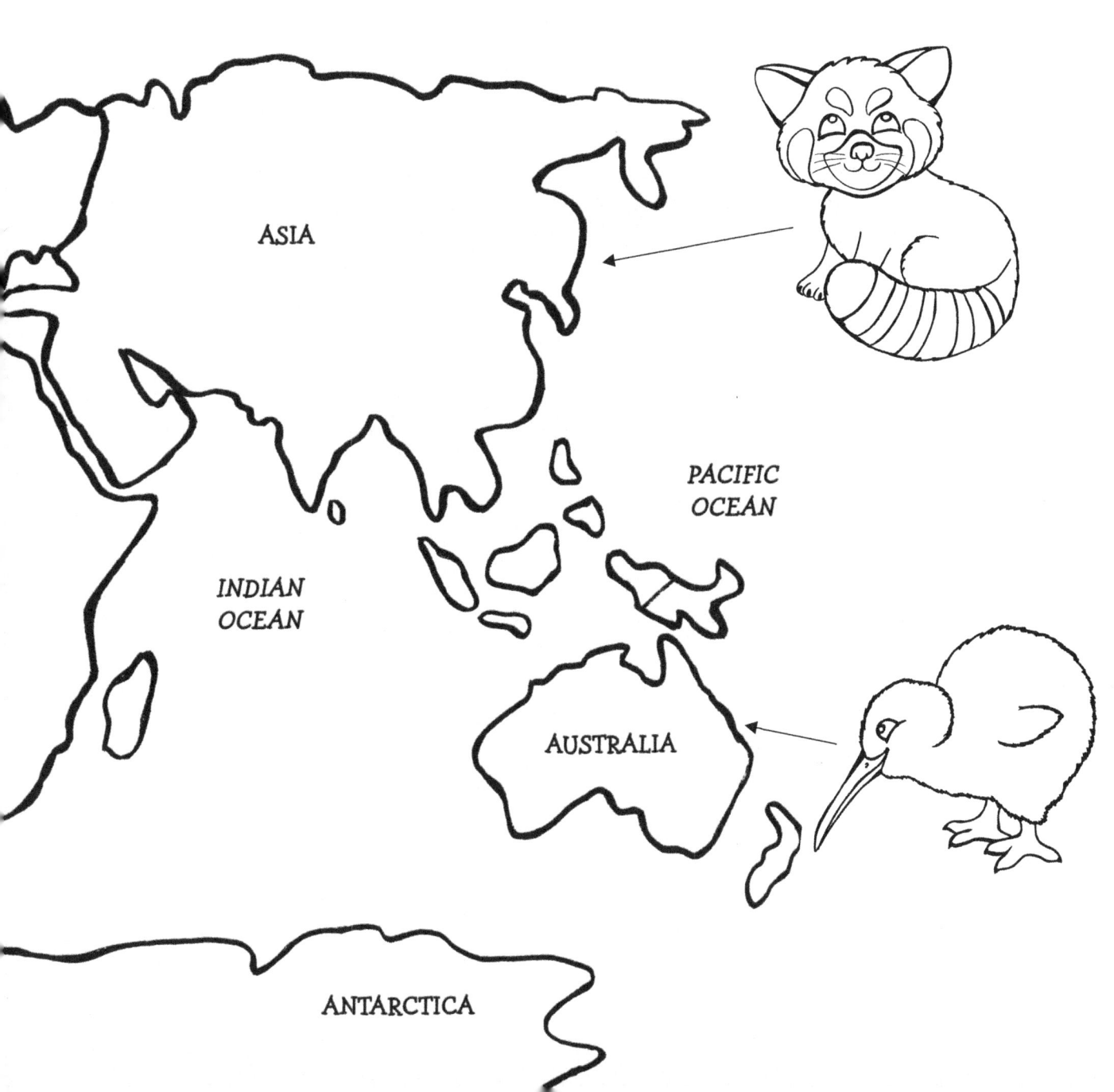

Thank You God for the continent of

North America!

North

America

Thank You God for the animals that live on the continent of North America!

Thank You God for Bald Eagles!

Bald Eagle

Bald Eagle

Bald Eagle

Thank You God for Pronghorns!

Pronghorn

Pronghorn

Pronghorn

Thank You God for Gray Foxes!

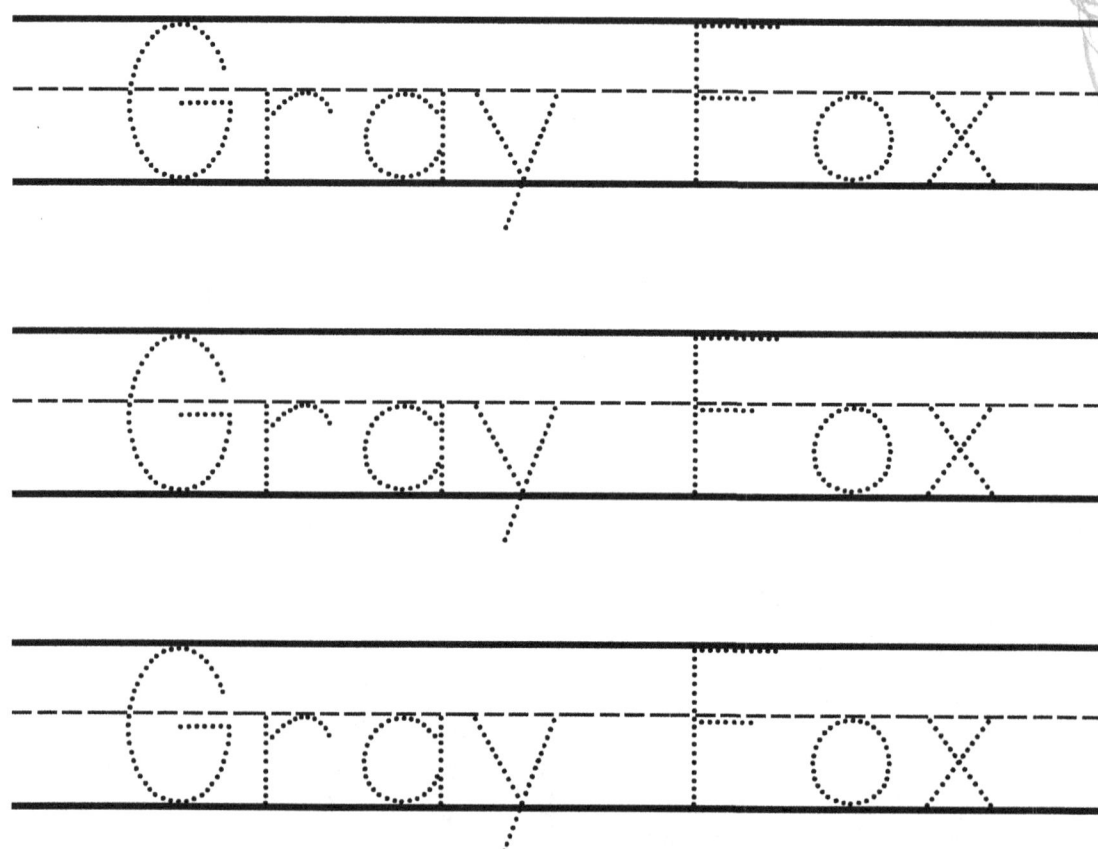

Thank You God for Desert Horned Lizards!

Lizard

Lizard

Lizard

Thank You God for American Bison!

Bison

Bison

Bison

Thank You God for Eastern Box Turtles!

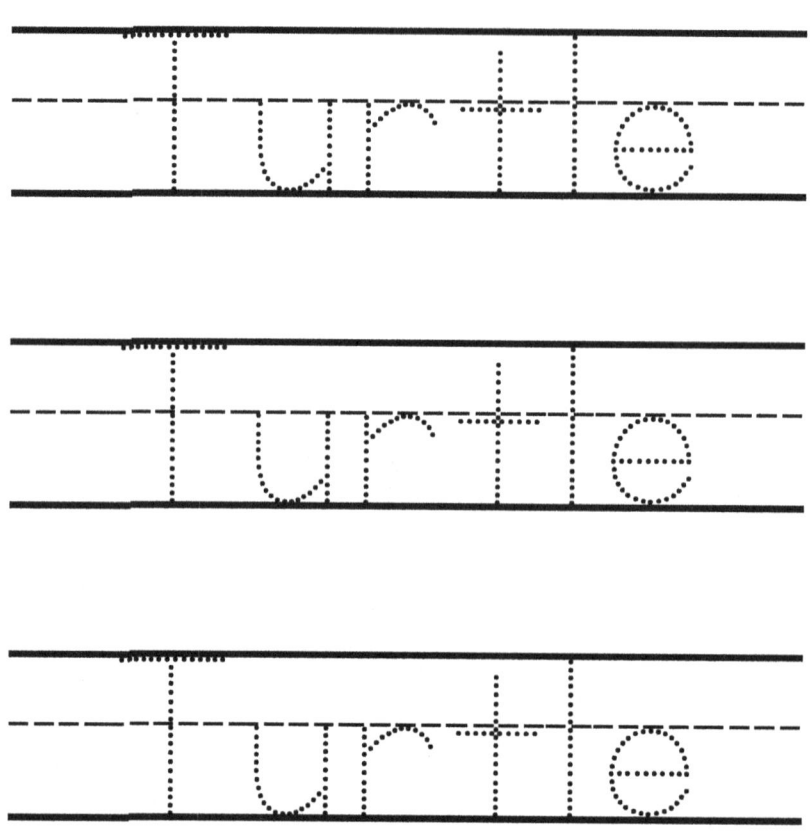

Thank You God for Bighorn Sheep!

Sheep

Sheep

Sheep

Thank You God for Pelicans!

Pelican

Pelican

Pelican

Thank You God for Bobcats!

Bobcat

Bobcat

Bobcat

Thank You God for California Quail!

Quail

Quail

Quail

Thank You God for the continent of

South America!

South

America

Thank You God for the animals that live on the continent of South America!

Thank You God for Lamas!

Lama

Lama

Lama

Thank You God for White-eared Opossums!

Opossum

Opossum

Opossum

Thank You God for Marmosets!

Marmoset

Marmoset

Marmoset

Thank You God for Golden Lion Tamarins!

Tamarin

Tamarin

Tamarin

Thank You God for Green Iguanas!

Iguana

Iguana

Iguana

Thank You God for Sloths!

Sloth

Sloth

Sloth

Thank You God for Pudu Deer!

Pudu

Pudu

Pudu

Thank You God for Toucans!

Toucan

Toucan

Toucan

Thank You God for Capybaras!

Capybara

Capybara

Capybara

Thank You God for Tapirs!

Tapir

Tapir

Tapir

Thank You God for the continent of

Europe!

Europe

Thank You God for the animals that live on the continent of Europe!

Thank You God for European Robins!

European

Robin

European

Robin

Thank You God for Western European Hedgehogs!

Hedgehog

Hedgehog

Hedgehog

Thank You God for the Eurasian Lynx!

Lynx

Lynx

Lynx

Thank You God for Brown Long-eared Bats!

Bat

Bat

Bat

Thank You God for the Garden Dormouse!

Dormouse

Dormouse

Dormouse

Thank You God for Fallow Deer!

Deer

Deer

Deer

Thank You God for Green Tree Frogs!

frog

frog

frog

Thank You God for Eurasian Shrews!

Shrew

Shrew

Shrew

Thank You God for European Pine Martens!

Marten

Marten

Marten

Thank You God for Northern Crested Newts!

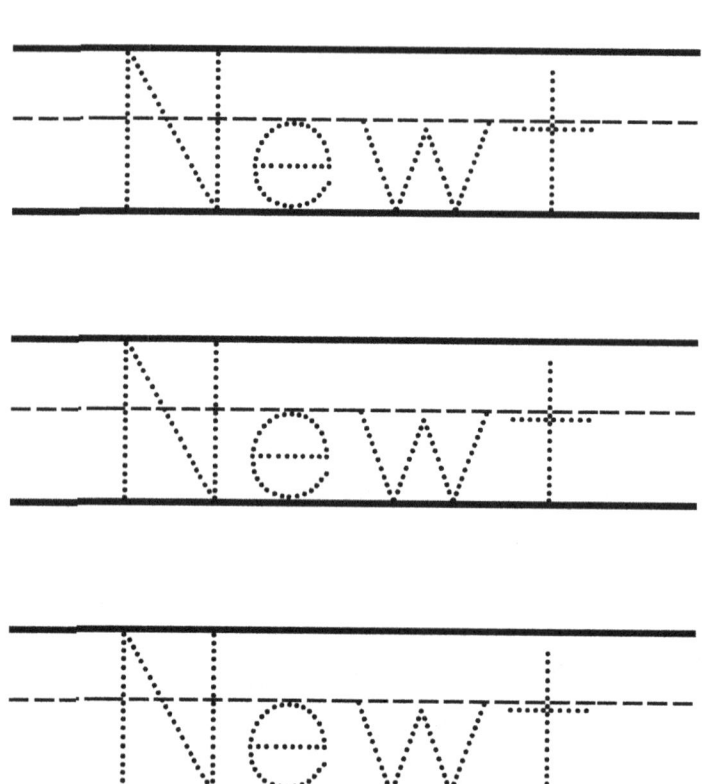

Thank You God for the animals that live on the continent of Asia!

Thank You God for Red Pandas!

Red Panda

Red Panda

Red Panda

Thank You God for Gibbons!

Gibbon

Gibbon

Gibbon

Thank You God for Tokay Geckos!

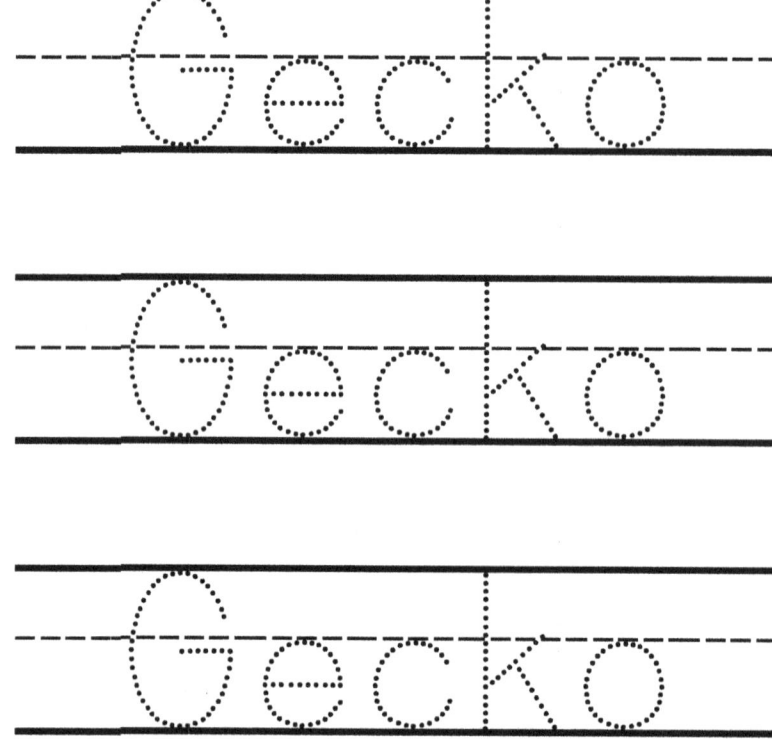

Thank You God for Green Magpies!

Magpie

Magpie

Magpie

Thank You God for Cloud Leopards!

Leopard

Leopard

Leopard

Thank You God for Pandas!

Panda

Panda

Panda

Thank You God for Tigers!

Tiger

Tiger

Tiger

Thank You God for Yaks!

Yak

Yak

Yak

Thank You God for Mandarin Ducks!

Duck

Duck

Duck

Thank You God for Orangutans!

Orangutan

Orangutan

Orangutan

Thank You God for the continent of

Africa!

Africa

Thank You God for the animals that live on the continent of Africa!

Thank You God for Cheetahs!

Cheetah

Cheetah

Cheetah

Thank You God for African Elephants!

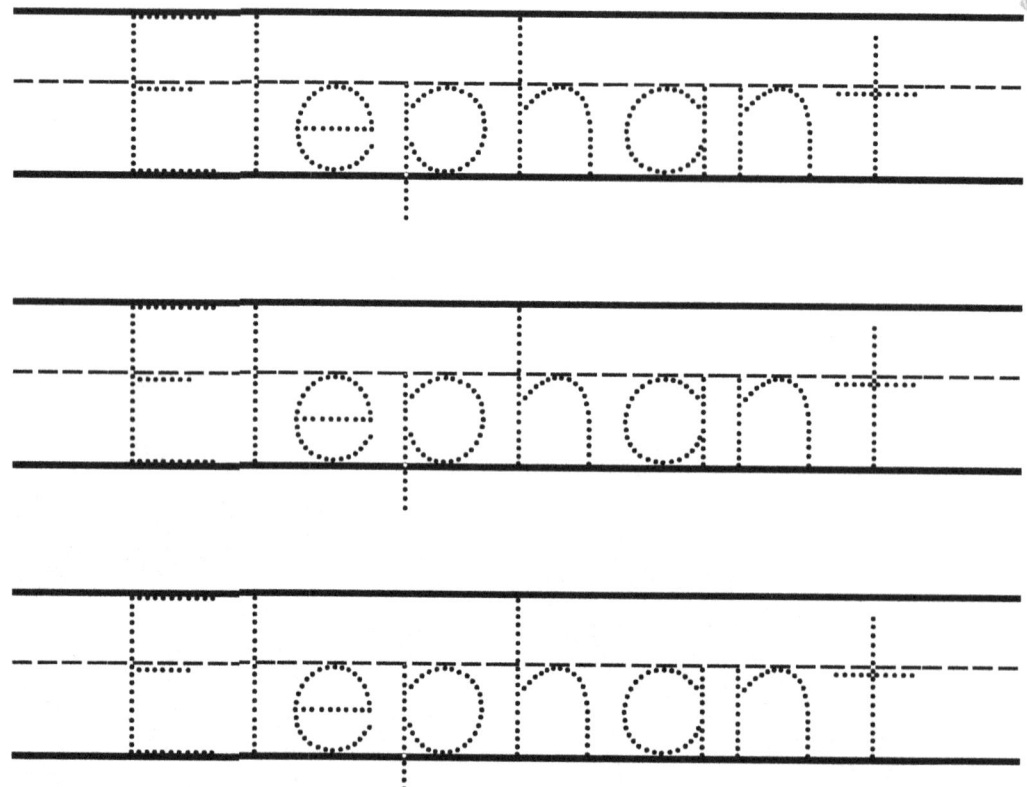

Thank You God for Lions!

Lion

Lion

Lion

Thank You God for Giraffes!

Giraffe

Giraffe

Giraffe

Thank You God for Lovebirds!

Lovebird

Lovebird

Lovebird

Thank You God for Zebras!

Zebra

Zebra

Zebra

Thank You God for Impalas!

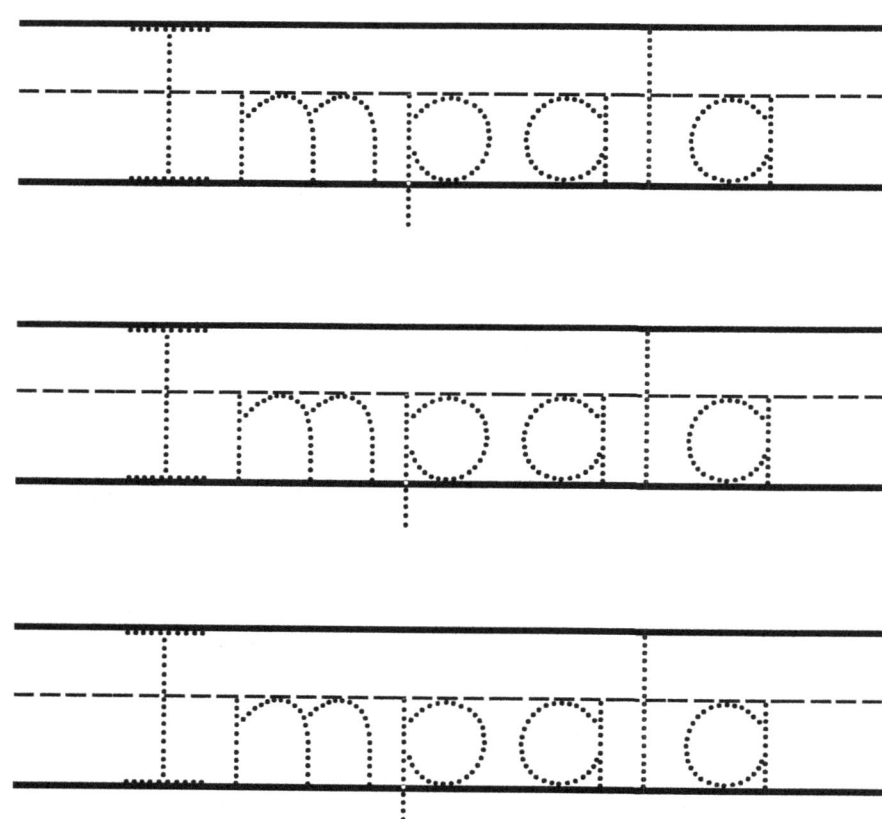

Thank You God for Hippos!

Hippo

Hippo

Hippo

Thank You God for Aardvarks!

Aardvark

Aardvark

Aardvark

Thank You God for Sand Foxes!

Sand Fox

Sand Fox

Sand Fox

Thank You God for the continent of Australia!

---Australia---

Thank You God for the animals that live on the continent of Australia!

Thank You God for Kiwis!

Kiwi

Kiwi

Kiwi

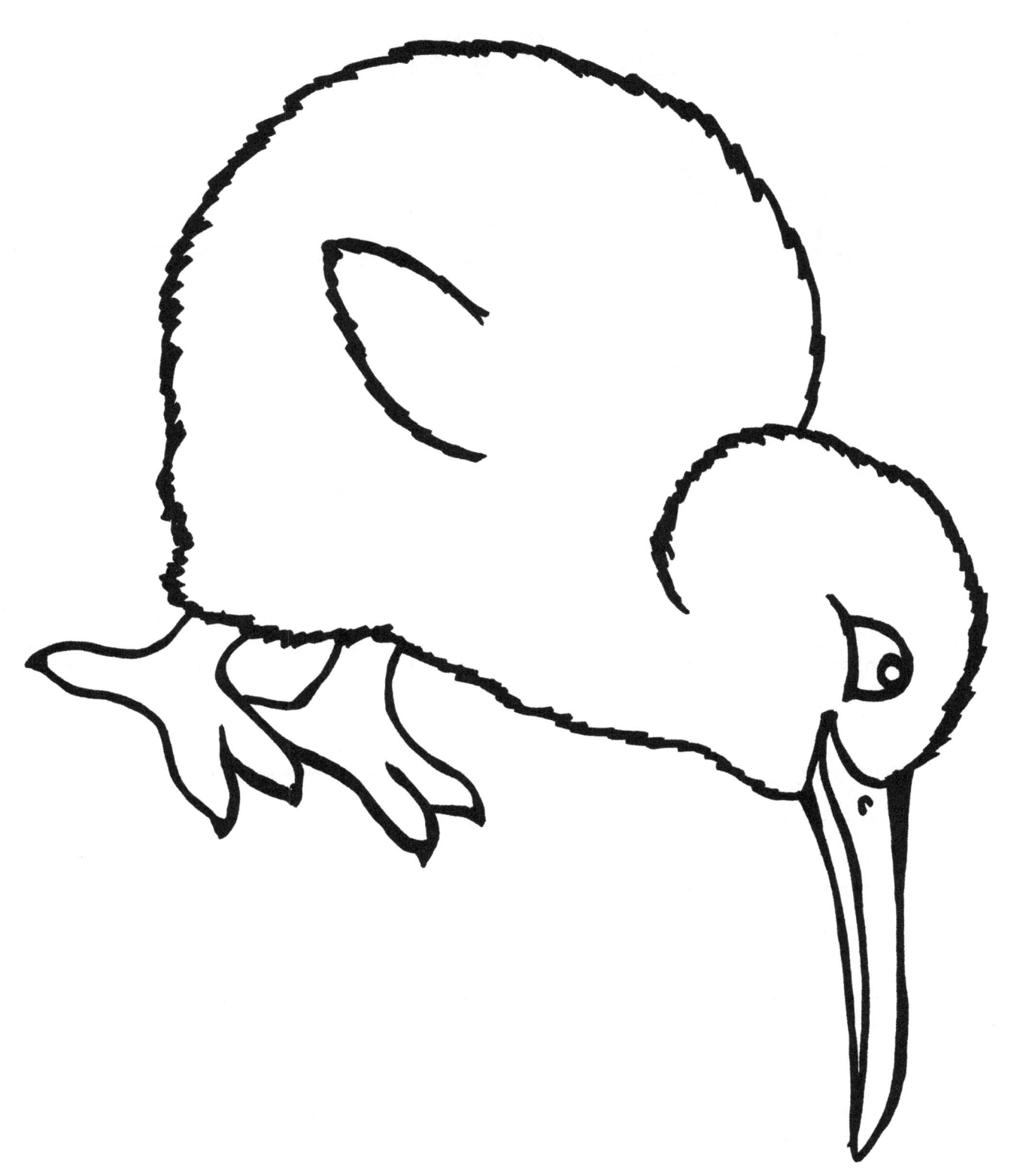

Thank You God for Cockatoos!

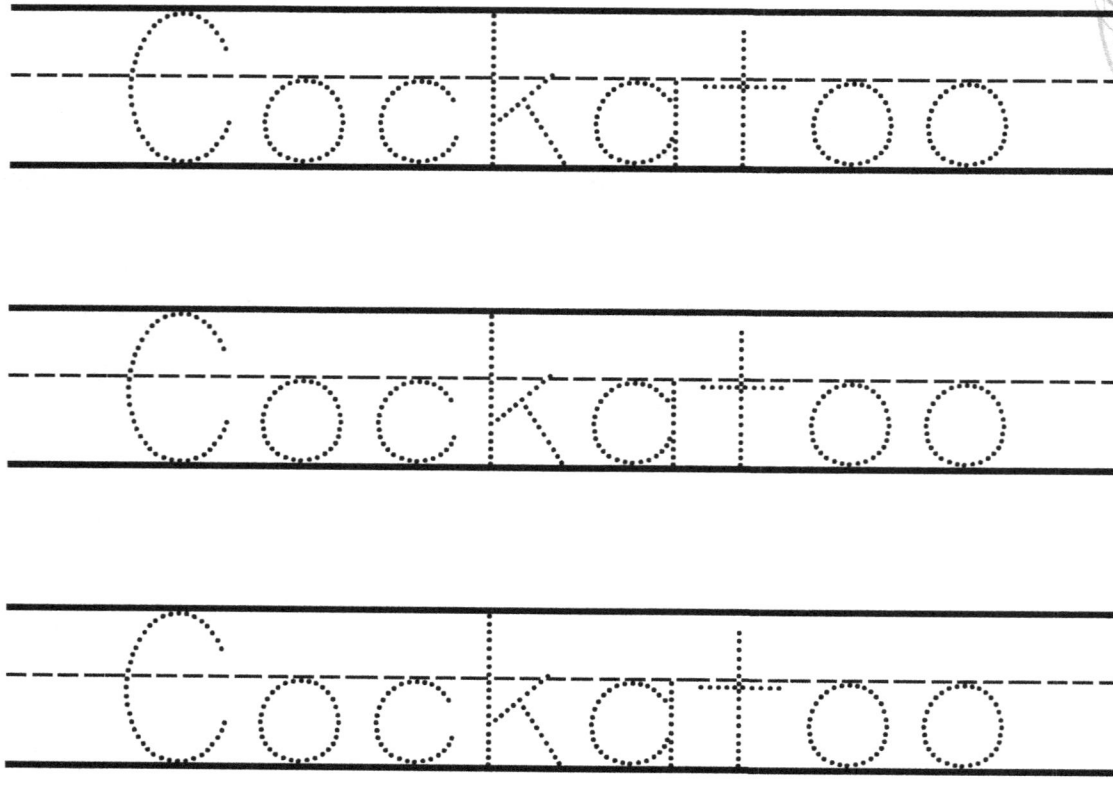

Thank You God for Kangaroos!

Kangaroo

Kangaroo

Kangaroo

Thank You God for Koalas!

Koala

Koala

Koala

Thank You God for Frilled Lizards!

Lizard

Lizard

Lizard

Thank You God for Platypuses!

Platypus

Platypus

Platypus

Thank You God for Echidnas!

Echidna

Echidna

Echidna

Thank You God for Sugar Gliders!

Sugar Glider

Sugar Glider

Sugar Glider

Thank You God for Wombats!

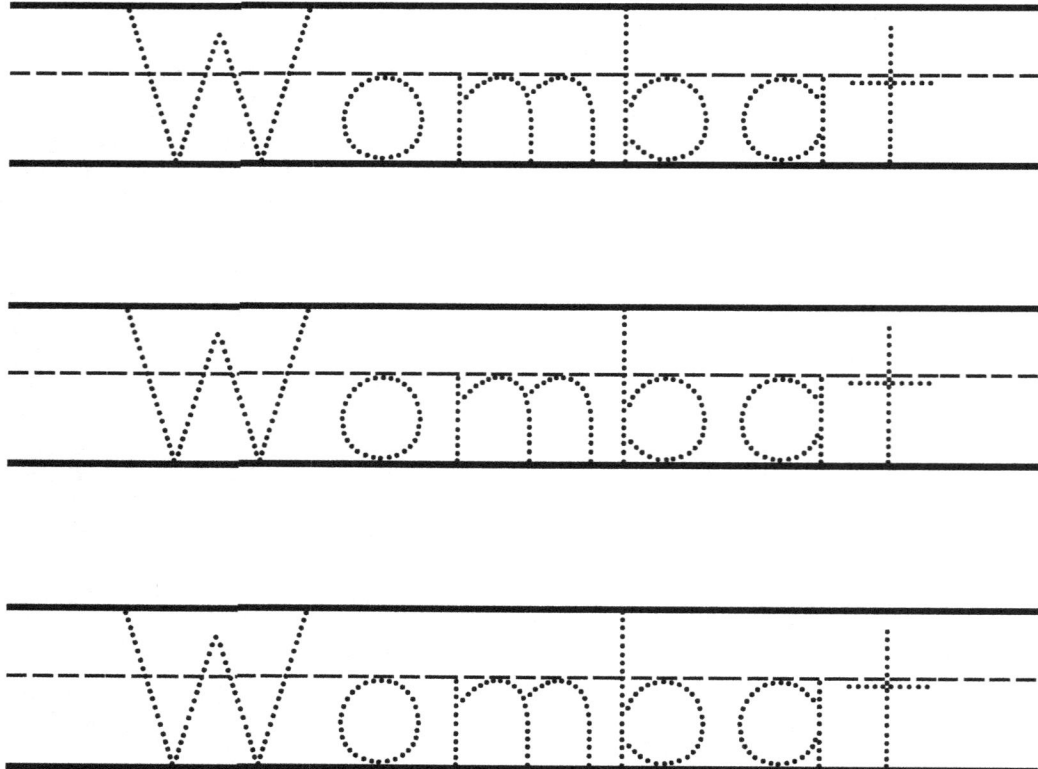

Thank You God for Australian Robins!

Australian

Robin

Australian

Robin

Thank You God for the continent of

Antarctica!

___Antarctica___

Thank You God for the animals that live on the continent of Antarctica!

Thank You God for Chinstrap Penguins!

Chinstrap

Penguin

Chinstrap

Penguin

Thank You God for Rockhopper Penguins!

Rockhopper

Penguin

Rockhopper

Penguin

Thank You God for Emperor Penguins!

Emperor

Penguin

Emperor

Penguin

Thank You God for Adelie Penguins!

Adelie

Penguin

Adelie

Penguin

Thank You God for Snowy Albatrosses!

Albatross

Albatross

Albatross

Thank You God for King Cormorants!

Cormorant

Cormorant

Cormorant

Thank You God for Snow Petrels!

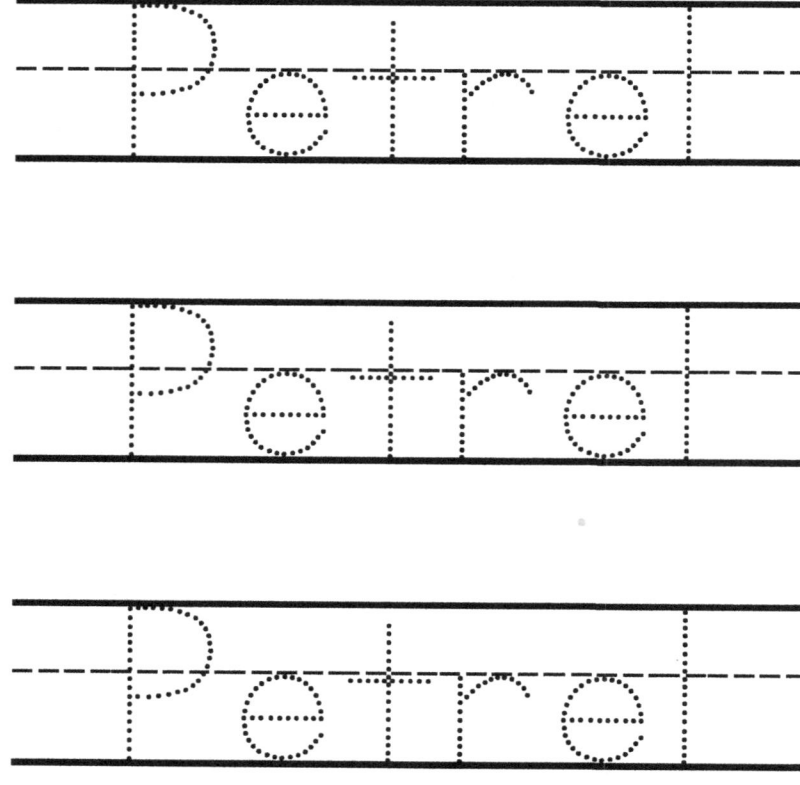

Thank You God for Common Seals!

Common Seal

Common Seal

Common Seal

Thank You God for Leopard Seals!

Leopard Seal

Leopard Seal

Leopard Seal

Thank You God for Elephant Seals!

Elephant Seal

Elephant Seal

Elephant Seal

Thank You God for all the Oceans!

Oceans

Thank You God for the animals that live in the Oceans!

Thank You God for Hammerhead Sharks!

Shark

Shark

Shark

Thank You God for Blue Whales!

Blue Whale

Blue Whale

Blue Whale

Thank You God for Orca Whales!

Orca Whale

Orca Whale

Orca Whale

Thank You God for Seahorses!

Seahorse

Seahorse

Seahorse

Thank You God for Swordfish!

Swordfish

Swordfish

Swordfish

Thank You God for Stingrays!

Stingray

Stingray

Stingray

Thank You God for Sea Turtles!

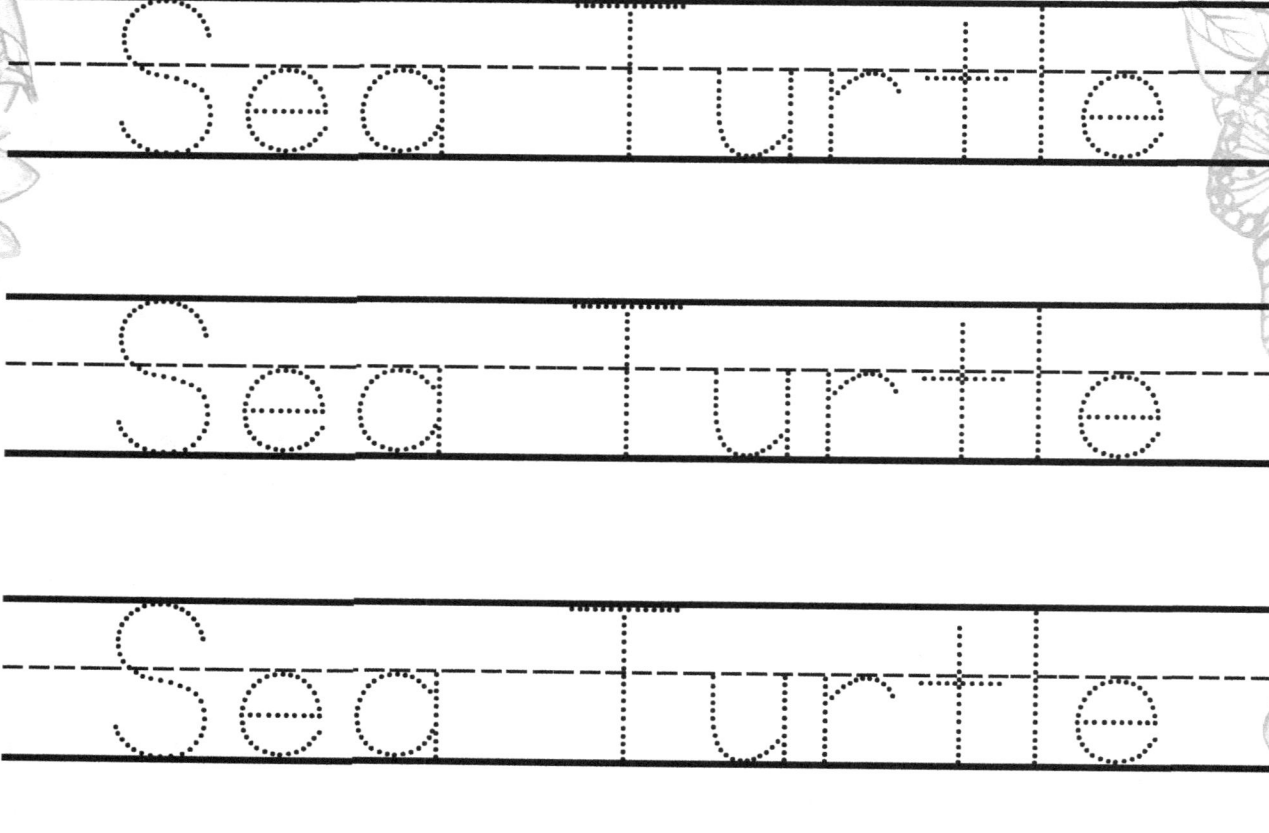

Sea Turtle

Sea Turtle

Sea Turtle

Thank You God for Jellyfish!

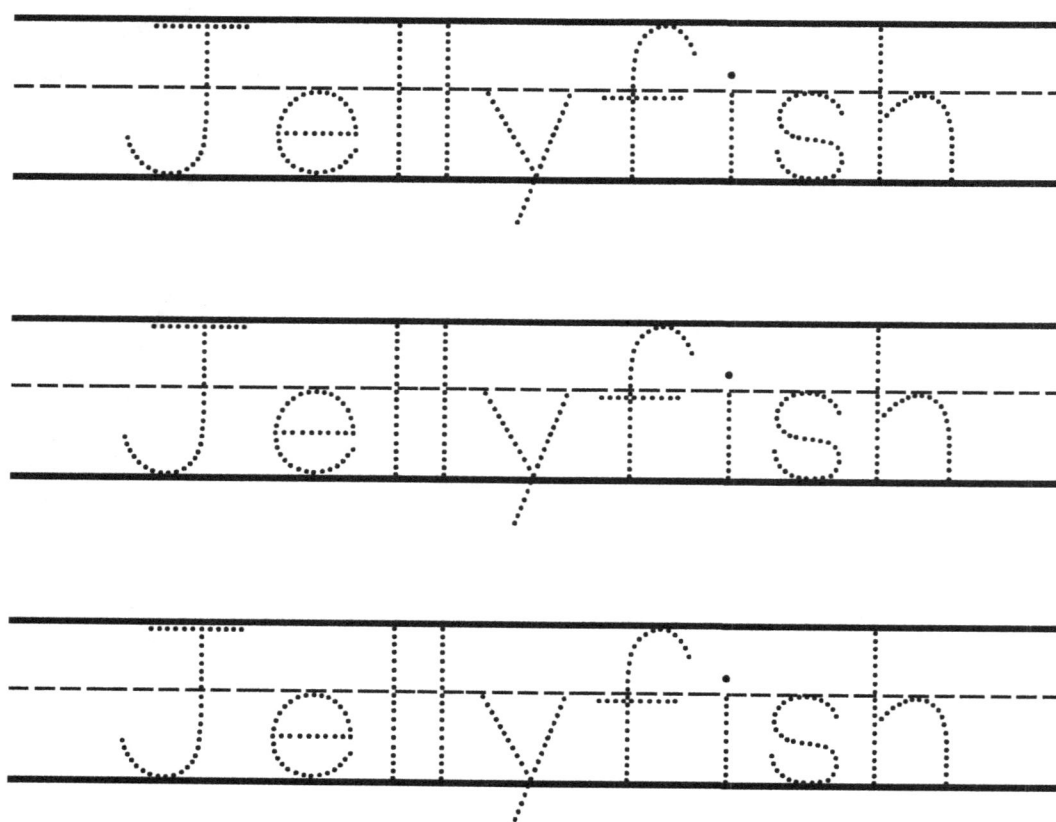

Thank You God for Crabs!

_ _ _ Crab _ _ _

_ _ _ Crab _ _ _

_ _ _ Crab _ _ _

Thank You God for Dolphins!

Dolphin

Dolphin

Dolphin

Hi, I am Dr. Diana Carle, the writer and illustrator behind this book, and I am delighted to share the wonder of God's creation with you! I earned my PhD in Entomology, a Bachelor of Science in Biology and Anthropology as well as a minor in the Classics, but my most impactful educational experience was the nature-based homeschool program in which I grew up. From exploring and sketching life along the pond's edge, to observing the miracle of butterfly metamorphosis, I learned at a young age that no classroom was as captivating as the one created by God in nature. As an adult, I have spent over 13 years in scientific research and STEM education, creating and delivering a wide range of hands-on science-based curricula for undergraduate, graduate, and adult professional education courses at Rutgers University. I served as a research associate on the Nurture thru Nature project, a grade 3 through 12 afterschool and summer program focused on bolstering students' scholastic performance and social development through active learning in nature. I also ran the state of New Jersey's mosquito control training and certification program where I educated health department personnel on responsible mosquito control which conserves both human and ecosystem health. I currently tutor students in Math, English, Art, and the Sciences. I also write and illustrate storybooks and educational materials while continuing to seek and learn from God in His creation through stewarding the wildlife in my backyard.

www.DoctorDianaCarle.com

Thank you so much for reading, I hope you experienced some of the wonder that learning in nature holds. If you are inspired to explore more about the natural world around us and how to use it as a learning resource, check out my other books, and join the mailing list by emailing me at:

DrDianaCarle@gmail.com

To Get Free Extras!

Title the email,
"Nature's Living Classroom"
And I'll send you a special
guide with activities for
learning in nature.

Made in United States
North Haven, CT
18 February 2023

32819718R00104